Every Soul Knows
Forget-Me-Not

Dedicated to...
all the wise souls in my life.

Published by Three Towers Press, an imprint of HenschelHAUS Publishing, Inc.
www.henschelHAUSbooks.com

ISBN: 978-1-59598-991-8

Printed in the United States of America

Mother, how my heart ached all my life to really know mine. But when I was a little girl, at the advanced age of four years, I was like other children; I too, had a mother. And she was beautiful. A mother who was happy, youthful and full of vitality!

I vividly recall how I sat on her bed and watched with childlike idolism her reflection in the dresser mirror. She stood erect in her favorite royal blue satin robe as she gazed at her reflection in the mirror. Then she brushed her long, dark brown wavy hair with even strokes as it hung in ripples down her back. Her clear deep blue eyes, under thick curled lashes, sparkled like stars. And her wide smile exposed perfect pearly-white even teeth.

In less than one week's time, life was all over for her. She'd been so alive with all the high hopes and unfulfilled desires she had for her future and that of her family. Then, suddenly from a heart attack, her twenty-seven brief years of life were snuffed out like a candle. Her new permanent address was now a heavenly mansion. God had called her to return to her Maker.

My heartbroken father immediately enlisted in the Armed Forces and left me in the custody of my maternal grandparents. The vivid memory of my mother was kept alive by my grandmother. My mother's portrait, mounted in an oval wooden frame, hung proudly on the parlor wall. There I was reminded of her image every day.

Her death happened in August. The days were extremely hot considering it was the northern part of Minnesota. The next day after the funeral services, I was taken to visit my mother's new grave by my grief-stricken grandmother. Grandma took me with her simply because she didn't know what else to do with me. And she was too engrossed in her recent sorrow to give it any serious thought.

"We must hurry," said Gram. "I want to catch that 9 o'clock trolley while it's still a little cool outside. It's getting hotter out there with each minute. Can't you walk just a little faster, child?"

"I'm coming." My short, spindly legs broke into a half–run in an effort to keep up with Gram's quick paces.

It was a good hour's ride before we arrived at our destination. The open window of the trolley created a draft and it helped to give some relief from the intense heat. The noise of their constant rattle with each churn of the trolley wheels didn't bother me. I'd sit quietly on the stiff cane seat while I watched out the screened window. And I enjoyed the slight breeze that blew gently across my childish face. I patiently looked out the window with all the curiosity of a small child. This routine became our everyday, as long as the weather permitted.

The time seemed to zoom by for me. I was contented with the trolley ride. Suddenly, Gram would stretch her arm over my head and pull on the cord that rang the bell. The dandelion-yellow trolley would sway from side to side then jerk to a screeching halt.

"Come, child." She moved mechanically like a robot. Then she picked up the wicker basket with her gardening tools and our lunch in it. Then she firmly grasped my tiny hand in hers and led me down the aisle.

I tagged at her heels with eager anticipation because the next thing on the agenda would be the bright spot of my day. This highlight was an unusual middle–aged gentleman. However, I never knew his name. He was a towering figure with a nice harmonious voice. This man was the conductor of the trolley who collected our fares. When it was time for us to descend, he swished me up in his sturdy arms and carried me down the steep steps of the trolley to safety. After he set me down on the sidewalk, he turned to Gram and said, "Be sure you take real good care of my best girl. I'll see you on your way home."

Then he kept waving his arm until the trolley pulled away. I waved too as I watched the trolley as it gained momentum and was out of sight as it continued to the end of the line. To me, he was my white knight in shining armor.

During our frequent trips, Gram stopped to pick up more fresh plants at the greenhouse. With a mother's tender loving care, she planted her choice selection of plants on my mother's freshly dug grave. Her stout form, still in jet-black mourning attire, dropped down to the ground on her plump knees. Then she leaned forward over the grave, as she patted, with her small pudgy hands, each particle of the good earth just the way she wanted it. To her, it had to be perfect.

The blistering hot sun beat unmercifully down on her bent figure and brought out beads of perspiration on her round flushed face. At the same time, her uncontrollable salted tears rolled down and smarted her crimson cheeks.

Each tiny Forget-Me-Not was chosen with the greatest care and planted to line the border of the grave. They set off the multi–colored pansies with their intricate patterns and the exquisite look of velvet. I was always encouraged to help.

As we worked, a terrible struggle went on inside me. I knew my mother was dressed in a brand-new white satin nightgown covered with white net. And that she rested her tired head on a fluffy white satin pillow. I realized my mother had been carefully placed in a pretty white bed. I was happy for her that she had such a beautiful place to sleep .

I remembered, too, that she'd been put into a deep hole in the ground in that pretty white bed. What my childish mind couldn't conceive was—when was she going to wake up? When was she going to get out of that beautiful white bed? To me, she'd had sufficient sleep. Not realizing I added to Gram's tremendous grief, I simply asked, "I wish my mama was here, don't you, Grandma? When is she going to wake up?"

Gram stopped working. She straightened up her thick body and sat back on her haunches. Her puffy, greenish-gray eyes were slits due to the many tears she had shed. She stared straight ahead. Her shoulders were pitifully sagged. Then in a half-whisper, like she was trying to convince herself it would really come true, she answered, "Someday, she will."

At the time, Grandma didn't offer me much conversation. Her troubled mind was occupied with her unbearable loss. But before Gram got through puttering around, I said, "Grandma, I'm hungry."

"I suppose you are, child. Time got away from me. I'll stop now and finish the planting later." Regretfully, she got up on her two feet. Then she brushed off, with a deliberate sweep of her hand, small pieces of the rich dirt that had clung to the bottom of her long black skirt.

"We'll have our lunch just as soon as we wash our hands."

I skipped lightly ahead of her on the path leading down to the water faucet.

In a shrill voice, Gram called out, "Wait for me!"

After we washed our hands, we sat down on the well-kept green grass close to the graveside while Gram studied and admired her own work of art. With her legs crossed Indian fashion under her, she dug into the basket of lunch she'd brought for us. She took out the peanut butter sandwiches, ginger cookies and the bananas. We got ice-cold water out of Lake Superior from the drinking fountain.

I know that Gram tried hard to be brave and to make these sorrowful occasions into a picnic for me. Somewhere along the line, she pulled on her abundant superhuman strength and managed to carry on the best she could in spite of a laden heart.

It was noon. It was time for us to catch the trolley back to town. During our regular visits, I'd learned to look forward to seeing my same conductor friend again. His kindness filled some of the void I felt. I longed for my mother's love and also the affection of my father. This thoughtful conductor was never too busy to be considerate of me. He deliberately walked down the aisle of the trolley and stopped at our seat. With a twinkle in his eye, he said to me, "I've a surprise just for you, young lady. Close your eyes and open your hand."

Then he'd reach into the pocket of his navy-blue uniform trimmed in gold braid and shabby from constant wear and take out my special surprise. His treat he carefully placed in my small hand.

With a grateful smile, I said, "Oh! Thank you." My delicate, uplifted face lit up like a Christmas tree with all the admiration I could possibly muster. I was always much happier when the piece of candy was peppermint. The taste of it was better to me than that of the horehound. But had he given me rat poison, I'd been glad to consume it, provided it came from him. No handsome young medieval knight, dressed in his finest ornate armor, had more adoration than my conductor friend. He was my very own Prince Charming.

When he carried me once again down the steps to safety, I knew we were headed on our way back to Grandma's house. With an upturned face and questioning gray eyes, I asked hopefully, "Grandma, when is my mama coming home? When is she coming to get me?"

At first, she answered vaguely, "One of these days."

After my repeated questioning, finally the poor woman out of desperation found the courage and said calmly, "Never."

Well, "never" meant to me that my mother would come and get me as soon as she could. I must wait. I didn't have any conception of how long **never** meant.

Each spring, Gram looked forward to once again planting her favorite plants on my mother's grave. However, after three years had passed, Gram was due for a dreadful shock. She received a letter from the cemetery officials that stated a regulation was passed by them that only cut flowers and plants placed in a specified container would be acceptable.

What a low blow! What cruelty! This new rule gave Gram a genuine bleeding heart. She'd been denied her rights. She was forced by them to make a supreme sacrifice by not being allowed to do her own planting. Never again would she have the personal satisfaction of giving of herself, with the working of the black soil with her two bare hands, and the comfort of her careful selection and arrangement of plants and flowers. And she desperately needed the self-expression of being able to turn them into her own creation of devoted love and beauty. Time marched on, leaving Gram with a deep scar over her heart that never did completely heal.

It was after I'd married and moved to another locality that I returned to my hometown. And then on one clear, refreshing summer day, I decided to visit my mother's grave. When I arrived at the cemetery, the large man-made pool at the entrance gate glittered like sparkling jewels as the mid–day sun reflected on it. Several white swans fluttered their outspread wings around   nonchalantly in the crystal cool water, unaware of my presence.

The wide gravel tarred road leading up to the family plot was lined with gigantic stately fir trees. They seemed to be much taller than I'd remembered. I could smell the familiar fragrance of pine they emitted.

As I continued, I came upon the natural lily pond surrounded by unhampered shrubbery. I stopped and gazed at it. The white water lilies with their large petals were securely nestled on their broad leaves. They appeared unconcerned as they floated on the still dark brown stagnant water. The pond hadn't changed. It looked the same to me as when I came with Gram so many moons ago. As I moved on, it brought back a flood of memories to me.

I meandered slowly along the road, then I remembered I must look for the immense white granite cross. Being in a Protestant cemetery, the cross was outstanding. In fact, it was the only one in the vast graveyard. The cross was my landmark. Gram had taught me to always look for it. I recalled how she wished with a deep passion to have a huge impressive monument like that to mark my mother's grave. But because she couldn't afford it, she resigned herself to an unpretentious, small foot stone. The cross was the identification marker of someone else, but to me, it meant I was getting closer to my destination. My mother's grave would be about fifty feet to the southeast of it.

I glanced up and viewed the once-familiar landmark. The cross was like meeting an old, staunch friend. It made me quicken my steps. Soon, I came to the spot where my dear mother's last remains were laid. I stood alone next to the grave site. Hot tears were streaming down my face. Like a flash of lightning, in my mind, I saw a petite child. Her dark brown hair was cut in a Buster Brown fashion. A girl who would many times sob herself to sleep, her head snuggled in her soft down feather pillow wet from her tears. I desperately yearned for my mother's guidance, devotion, and love.

In a solemn manner, I gazed down at the grass-covered grave. I was in for a pleasant surprise. To my astonishment, tiny blue forget–me–nots were sparsely scattered around the edge of her grave.

Then I asked myself if these tiny blue flowers had grown, despite difficult obstacles, because of the tender love given them in their planting? Or had they refused to surrender to the order of death so they would be able to give me a personal message?

After giving it serious thought, I believed my mother had reached out from behind the veil of death. For to me, it was as though she were saying, "Forget–Me–Not."

The End

For Notes and Thoughts

For Notes and Thoughts

For Notes and Thoughts

For Notes and Thoughts

For Notes and Thoughts